This Autograph Book Belongs To:

All rights reserved. No part of this publication may be reproduced, stored in a retrieval system, or transmitted in any form or by any means, electronic, mechanical, photocopying, or otherwise without the prior permission of the copyright owner.

Copyright © 2020

Who is Dr. Furr?

Dr. Furr is shy, yet a playful cat. But the truth is, he does not like to be known just as a cat.

He prefers to be known and called as "Dr. Furr." Because, why not?

He is quite knowledgeable and smart.
He loves hugs and cuddles. He also roams around (and travels) a lot.

What else he does?
In his free time, he writes books (mostly kids' series) and creates collectibles.

If you see him around or run into him, say "Hi, Dr. Furr!"

Did you know that there are other books in Dr. Furr series?

Don't forget to collect those.
Let Dr. Furr know that you love his series.

Just type the ASIN number in Amazon Marketplace.

ASIN: B0863TWDS8

ASIN: B085KR4672

How to Use this Autograph Book?

- This is a blank autograph and photo book ready for you to collect autographs and pictures of your favorite person, friends, tv/film stars, Disney or cartoon characters, or anyone you love.

- The pictures will go on the left and the autograph will go on the right side of the page.

- Make this a collection space of all the autographs and photos.

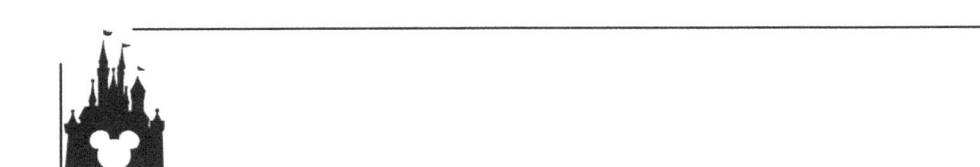

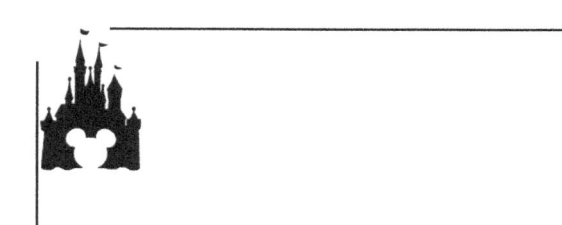

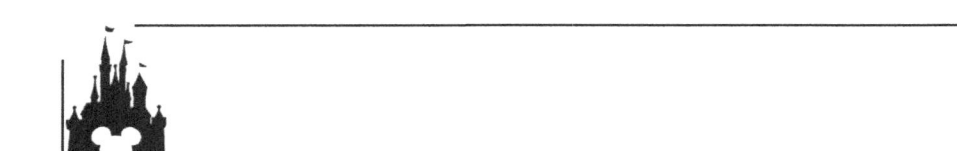

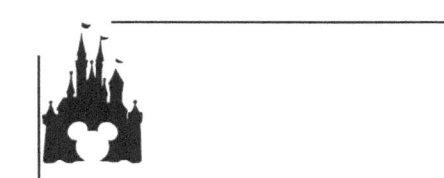

Made in the USA
Monee, IL
14 November 2021